CCNA Cyber Ops
(210-250 & 210-255)
Ultimate
Practice Exam

By:
Charles Judd
CCNA R&S and Security | BS Network Security

KEVIN WALLACE
TRAINING, LLC

Introduction

Thanks so much for your purchase of the **CCNA Cyber Ops (210-250 and 210-255) Practice Exam**. Before diving into the questions, let's talk about the philosophy behind these questions. First of all, we believe that brain dumps for exams, which you might find on the Internet, hurt our industry. They help people without an understanding of the technology become certified, which devalues the certifications that we've worked so hard to earn.

Here's how we're combatting that. I've dramatically undercut the prices of the big brain dump vendors. Also, I've created a set of questions that addresses the topics found on the exam (according to Cisco's exam blueprint), and I've thoroughly explained why the correct answer is correct. So, this practice exam is not an attempt to have you memorize answers, but rather, the goal is to help you understand the technology at a deeper level and confirm your understanding of the various exam topic areas.

I salute you for your integrity in choosing a brain-dump-free practice exam.

Charles Judd

Kevin Wallace Training, LLC

Video Resources

To supplement your studies, Charles Judd has created a video training series that covers key topics from the CCNA Cyber Ops SECFND 210-250 and SECOPS 210-255 exams. The training includes 137 individual videos with a run time of over 10 Hours. All of the training videos are available for downloadable offline usage.

You can sign up for a free preview course here:

https://kwtrain.com/cyberops-preview

Learn more about the **Cisco CCNA Cyber Ops Video Training Series** here:

https://kwtrain.com/cyberops

Questions

1. In a typical switch, where is information about Layer 2 addressing stored?

   a. L2 Table
   b. CAM Table
   c. MAC Address Table
   d. Routing Table

2. Which protocol is used to provide quick, automatic addressing within a network?

   a. ARP
   b. DNS
   c. IP
   d. DHCP

3. What is the defining characteristic of a hub?

   a. They repeat information and transmit to peers
   b. They make intelligent forwarding decisions based on Layer 3 addressing
   c. They are more cost effective to deploy
   d. They use a MAC address table for frame switching

4. Which category of Wireless Access Points (WAPs) are able to handle both real-time and management functions?

   a. Lightweight Access Points
   b. Autonomous Access Points
   c. Wireless LAN Controllers
   d. Wireless Repeaters

5. Which of the following is not one of the values that comprises the 5-Tuple information found in NetFlow?

   a. Source Port
   b. Destination IP
   c. Protocol
   d. MAC Address

6. Which of the following is true in regard to NetFlow vs. full-packet capture techniques?

    a. NetFlow requires more storage
    b. They utilize the same bandwidth
    c. NetFlow is more cost effective
    d. Full-packet capture is faster

7. Which form of Network Address Translation (NAT) allows for connections to be initiated bidirectionally?

    a. Static NAT
    b. Dynamic NAT
    c. Policy NAT
    d. Port Address Translation

8. In which mode of deployment for a Cisco Web Security Appliance (WSA) are the other network clients aware of the device's presence?

    a. Transparent Proxy Mode
    b. Explicit Proxy Mode
    c. Web Cache Mode
    d. Proxy Redirect Mode

9. Which CVSS version 3 metric measures the level of access that an attacker needs in order to successfully launch an attack?

    a. Attack Complexity
    b. User Interaction
    c. Attack Vector
    d. Privileges Required

10. A user on your network receives an email with a malicious attachment, but there is no indication that the file was interacted with in any way. Which category of the Diamond Model of Intrusion does this activity fall under?

    a. Reconnaissance
    b. Installation

c. Exploitation

d. Delivery

11. Which of the following is true in regard to the Principle of Least Privilege?

    a. It does not apply to managers

    b. It is essentially the same as Separation of Duties

    c. All users should have minimum access

    d. It is only necessary in regard to employees

12. What is defined as any potential danger to an asset within an organization?

    a. Exploit

    b. Threat

    c. Malicious Actor

    d. Threat Agent

13. What is identified as an active entity used to place resource requests for access to passive entities?

    a. Subject

    b. Object

    c. Control

    d. User

14. In which phase of the access control process is a user required to prove their identity?

    a. Identification

    b. Authentication

    c. Authorization

    d. Accounting

15. Which type of users are ultimately responsible for the overall security of an asset?

    a. System Owners

    b. Security Administrators

    c. Senior Management

    d. End Users

16. Which of the following methods of authentication could be considered examples of authentication by characteristic?

   a. Server room key
   b. Passphrase
   c. RFID card
   d. Fingerprints

17. Which of the following is a feature of a typical Mobile Device Management (MDM) solution?

   a. Call tracking
   b. PIN code enforcement
   c. Cloud backups
   d. Speed dial

18. Which type of penetration test involves a case where no information about networks and systems are provided beforehand?

   a. Black box testing
   b. White box testing
   c. Gray box testing
   d. Red hat testing

19. Which of the following is not considered to be an advantage of Security Information and Event Management (SIEM) systems?

   a. Command line interface
   b. Ability to correlate redundant log entries
   c. Log search functionality
   d. Lower administrative overhead

20. During which phase of the patch management process would you take into account any additional mitigation measures needed during rollout?

   a. Identification
   b. Prioritization

c. Evaluation

d. Updating

21. Which of the following is an example of an asymmetrical algorithm commonly used in our modern networks?

    a. DES

    b. 3DES

    c. AES

    d. RSA

22. Which of the following is not considered to be a deprecated hash function?

    a. SHA-1

    b. SHA-2

    c. MD5

    d. DSA

23. Which of the following values would not commonly be found within a digital certificate?

    a. Domain name

    b. Public key

    c. DNS Server

    d. CA Signature

24. Which method of IPsec implementation includes payload encryption?

    a. ESP

    b. AH

    c. VPN

    d. DSL

25. Which of the following VPN protocols provides data integrity, authentication, and encryption?

    a. L2TP

    b. GRE

    c. SSL

d. MPLS

26. Which of the following is not part of the IKE Phase 1 policy set that is needed for an ISAKMP SA negotiation?

    a. Encryption
    b. Key
    c. Group
    d. Lifetime

27. Which step of VPN negotiation creates an IPsec Security Association (SA) when completed?

    a. Main Mode
    b. Aggressive Mode
    c. IKE Phase 1
    d. IKE Phase 2

28. Which type of SSL VPN requires a browser-based connection method?

    a. Thin Client VPN
    b. Clientless VPN
    c. Site-to-Site VPN
    d. Full Tunnel VPN

29. Which of the following statements are true in regard to memory stacks and heaps?

    a. Heaps can allocate blocks of memory at any time
    b. Stacks can allocate blocks of memory at any time
    c. Stacks are best for dynamic memory allocation
    d. Heaps are best for static memory allocation

30. What is the best description of a handle function in Windows OS?

    a. API programmers change handles
    b. Handles grant access rights to the OS
    c. Hides real memory addresses from API users
    d. Pointers and handles are the same concept

31. In Windows, what are defined as a long-running application which operate in its own session?

    a. Registry Key
    b. Program
    c. WMI
    d. Service

32. Which of the following is considered to be a function of the Windows Registry?

    a. Software registration
    b. Loading device drivers
    c. Backing up OS settings
    d. Collecting logging information

33. In UNIX environments, what is the name of the first process started during the boot sequence?

    a. Parent
    b. Init
    c. Daemon
    d. Orphan

34. What type of process happens when a parent process is terminated, but the child process continues to function on its own?

    a. Step-Parent Process
    b. Zombie Process
    c. Orphan Process
    d. Daemon Process

35. Which is the following is true about Daemon processes?

    a. They run in the background
    b. They run in the foreground
    c. They manage OS upgrades
    d. They cannot be terminated

36. Which severity of Syslog would indicate something such as a kernel panic?

    a. Level 10
    b. Level 7
    c. Level 3
    d. Level 0

37. What type of malicious software typically comes in the form of malicious code inserted into a legitimate application?

    a. Worm
    b. Keylogger
    c. Ransomware
    d. Logic Bomb

38. Which of the following is Cisco's recommended solution for endpoint protection?

    a. Cisco WSA
    b. Cisco ESA
    c. Cisco AMP
    d. Cisco ASA

39. What is another name for a host-based firewall?

    a. Next-Generation Firewall
    b. Personal Firewall
    c. Standard Firewall
    d. Stateful Firewall

40. What is the definition of a graylist item?

    a. Entities or actions not yet deemed to be either malicious or allowed
    b. Authorized hosts, applications, services, or email addresses
    c. Unauthorized hosts, applications, services, or email addresses
    d. Entities or actions that should be ignored completely

41. Which type of security device has the ability to actively interact with network traffic and drop anything that has been deemed malicious?

    a. WPS
    b. IDS
    c. IPS
    d. ESA

42. Why is it important to enable the Network Time Protocol (NTP) on all devices within the network, particularly those from which logs are being collected?

    a. To make sure OS updates are applied
    b. To make sure logs are accurate
    c. For certificate management
    d. To synchronize network changes

43. Under which directory do most UNIX-based systems keep logs?

    a. /var/log
    b. /var/syslog
    c. /var/lastlog
    d. /var/auth

44. Which of the following is not a useful attribute that you would want to collect during endpoint monitoring?

    a. Service pack data
    b. Application logs
    c. DNS hostnames
    d. Running processes

45. Which Cisco product offers a solution to the challenge of identifying attack information where Network Address Translation (NAT) is deployed?

    a. Cisco AMP for Endpoints
    b. Cisco ASA with Firepower
    c. Intrusion Prevention System
    d. Cisco Lancope Stealthwatch

46. Which of the following is a common method for data exfiltration that uses data transfer via a protocol that is not designed for carrying data?

   a. Port Address Translation
   b. DNS Tunneling
   c. Backdoors
   d. Trojan Horse

47. Which of the following would not be a red flag in regard to suspicious host activity on a network?

   a. High bandwidth usage for a specific endpoint
   b. Network activity at strange times
   c. Peer-to-peer communication
   d. Sluggish performance on the host

48. What is Tor primarily used for?

   a. Local drive encryption
   b. Remote host management
   c. Anonymous browsing
   d. VPN functionality

49. Which of the following intelligence gathering sources would not be considered a passive reconnaissance method?

   a. Port scan
   b. DNS lookup
   c. Search engines
   d. Social media

50. Which type of attack utilizes networks of compromised hosts to render target networks or systems unavailable?

   a. Zombies
   b. DoS
   c. DDoS

d. Ransomware

51. Which tenet of the CIA triad is encryption used to protect?

    a. Confidentiality
    b. Integrity
    c. Availability
    d. Authorization

52. Which of the following is not included in the DREAD threat modeling methodology?

    a. Damage Potential
    b. Reconnaissance
    c. Exploitability
    d. Affected Users

53. Which of the following is not included in the STRIDE threat modeling methodology?

    a. Tampering
    b. Reputation
    c. Denial of Service
    d. Elevation of Privilege

54. What is the sum of all pathways or means by which an attacker can gain access to a resource?

    a. Attack Vector
    b. Entry Point
    c. Injection Point
    d. Attack Surface

55. What is defined as conditions that must exist beyond an attacker's control in order to exploit a vulnerability?

    a. Availability
    b. Exposure
    c. Complexity
    d. Vector

56. Which CVSS metric measures the need for actions to be taken from someone other than the threat actor?

    a. User Interaction
    b. Privileges Required
    c. Assistance Vector
    d. Scope Change

57. Which type of forensic investigation is categorized as a typical corporate investigation?

    a. Individual Investigation
    b. Private Investigation
    c. Public Investigation
    d. Criminal Investigation

58. In regard to cyber forensics, what is defined as the process of searching through unallocated hard drive space in order to attempt deleted file recovery?

    a. Write Blocking
    b. Disk Imaging
    c. Data Carving
    d. Drive Hashing

59. What is the term for a basic unit that an Operating System allocated processor time toward?

    a. Service
    b. Job
    c. Thread
    d. Object

60. Which of the following would not be considered a common cyber-attack artifact element?

    a. IP address
    b. URL
    c. Hashes
    d. VPN

61. In terms of alerting, what does it mean when there is malicious activity within our systems being seen as legitimate actions?

    a. False Positives
    b. False Negatives
    c. True Negatives
    d. True Positives

62. Which of the following is not a common type of evasion technique used against traditional IDS and IPS?

    a. Jumbo Frames
    b. Fragmentation
    c. Encryption
    d. Low Bandwidth

63. Which protocol is used by IPFIX for transport of packets?

    a. SSL
    b. SCTP
    c. HTTPS
    d. ESP

64. Which version of NetFlow is the IPFIX flow standard based upon?

    a. NetFlow Version 9
    b. NetFlow Version 8
    c. NetFlow Version 7
    d. NetFlow Version 5

65. What does the National Institute of Security and Technology (NIST) define as an observable occurrence in a system or a network?

    a. Violation
    b. Incident
    c. Event
    d. Breach

66. What does the National Institute of Security and Technology (NIST) define as a violation or imminent threat of violation of computer security policies, acceptable use policies, or standard security practices?

    a. Security Event
    b. Breach
    c. Negative Event
    d. Security Incident

67. Which of the following is not part of the Incident Response Life Cycle as outlined by NIST?

    a. Preparation
    b. Detection and Analysis
    c. System Backups
    d. Post-Incident Activity

68. Which of the following is considered to be a main goal of Computer Security Incident Response Teams (CSIRTs)?

    a. Hiring penetration testers
    b. Monitoring firewall rules
    c. Minimize damage to assets
    d. Deploy intrusion prevention systems

69. Which type of team is typically formed by hardware and software vendors to investigate, resolve, and disclose security vulnerabilities in their own products.

    a. PSIRTs
    b. CERTs
    c. CSIRTs
    d. FIRSTs

70. The PCI DSS framework was developed to protect which of the following?

    a. Electronic healthcare information
    b. Financial Data
    c. Tax Returns

d. Voter Registration

71. Which of the following is not a phase of the Cyber Kill Chain?

    a. Recovery
    b. Installation
    c. Exploitation
    d. Reconnaissance

72. In the Diamond Model of Intrusion, what is identified as the target that is being exploited?

    a. Infrastructure
    b. Adversary
    c. Vulnerability
    d. Victim

73. What kind of forensic evidence is considered to be the most reliable when attempting to arrive at an analytical assertion?

    a. Corroborative
    b. Indirect
    c. Direct
    d. Circumstantial

74. Which tenet of the CIA triad refers to the trustworthiness and veracity of information?

    a. Confidentiality
    b. Integrity
    c. Availability
    d. Encryption

75. During which phase of the Cyber Kill Chain is the adversary actively in the network, beginning to achieve objectives?

    a. Weaponization
    b. Installation
    c. Delivery
    d. Actions

76. What does PHI stand for?

    a. Private Health Information
    b. Protected Health Information
    c. Personal Health Information
    d. Private Health Insurance

77. What is the measure of the actual amount of data traveling through a network?

    a. Throughput
    b. Bandwidth
    c. Speed
    d. Latency

78. In regard to baseline network metrics, what might be an indicator of a potentially underutilized area of a network topology?

    a. Peaks
    b. Valleys
    c. Dips
    d. Latency

79. What type of memory gets allocated during compile time by a program?

    a. Static
    b. Startup
    c. Random
    d. Dynamic

80. Which of the following is not one of the three general types of forensic evidence?

    a. Best Evidence
    b. Corroborating Evidence
    c. Digital Evidence
    d. Circumstantial Evidence

81. What common type of attack is stored on the web server itself, and is accomplished through submitting input to forms which populate database fields, such as comment boxes or message boards?

    a. Reflected XSS
    b. SQL Injection
    c. Phishing
    d. Persistent XSS

82. What is the Syslog severity level for debug messages?

    a. 2
    b. 3
    c. 7
    d. 5

83. What is defined as a set of rules related to encrypting or decrypting data?

    a. Key
    b. Cipher
    c. Algorithm
    d. Encryption

84. Which of the following is not an important consideration under the Sarbanes-Oxley (SOX) Act framework?

    a. C-Level employees must certify financial records
    b. External auditors must perform annual audits
    c. Public disclosure of changes to financial conditions
    d. Annual corporate shareholder meetings

85. Which type of solution is used as a collection of procedures detailing security operations, such as identifying, containing, and removing threats?

    a. Runbook
    b. Procedure Guide
    c. Instruction Manual
    d. Policy

86. What type of network-related symptom is defined as a periodical, outbound connection that comes from a compromised host?

    a. Beaconing
    b. Homing
    c. Pinging
    d. Calling

87. Which type of password attack tool uses a large database with hash values pre-matched to plain text outputs?

    a. Dictionary Attack
    b. Brute-Force Attack
    c. Rainbow Table Attack
    d. Key-Logger Attack

88. Which type of common wireless attack uses a rogue access point that appears to be legitimate, typically placed in a public area with open authentication?

    a. Eavesdropping
    b. Evil Twin Attack
    c. MAC Spoofing
    d. Management Jacking

89. Which of the following procedures would not be helpful when collecting data for measuring network throughput?

    a. SPAN port configuration
    b. NetFlow collector data
    c. Gateway firewall statistics
    d. Operating System versions

90. Which analysis type is based on known facts obtained about the incident, breach, or infection?

    a. Behavioral
    b. Contextual

    c. Probabilistic

    d. Deterministic

91. Which of the following is not considered to be one of the important meta-features used in the Diamond Model of Intrusion?

    a. Timestamp

    b. Result

    c. Password

    d. Methodology

92. Which of the following would be an example of an external entity that you may be required to communicate with during the investigation and resolution of a security incident?

    a. Media

    b. Managers

    c. Employees

    d. Financial Advisors

93. Which of the following data artifacts are not commonly shown in NetFlow records?

    a. Source Ports

    b. Usernames

    c. Destination IP Addresses

    d. Protocols

94. NIST SP 800-61 outlines the important phases of a security incident, including the post-incident activity phase. Which of the following procedures is not considered to be part of this post-mortem?

    a. Discussing lessons learned

    b. Retaining evidence

    c. Pinpointing attacking hosts

    d. Using collected data

95. When encapsulating data using the OSI model as a reference, the MAC address of the sending and receiving hosts are identified at which layer?

a. Layer 4
b. Layer 3
c. Layer 2
d. Layer 7

96. Which of the following is not a common message exchanged during the four-step DHCP address negotiation between server and client?

a. DHCPDISCOVER
b. DHCPOFFER
c. DHCPREQUEST
d. DHCPRENEW

97. Which type of device sits between protected and unprotected networks in order to terminate connections as a "middle-man" between the two?

a. Proxy
b. Firewall
c. IPS
d. Relay

98. Which of the following is not an example of a well-known symmetric-key algorithm?

a. 3DES
b. Blowfish
c. RSA
d. AES

99. In Linux, which of the following commands is used to change group ownership of a particular file?

a. CHmod
b. CHgrp
c. CHown
d. CHedit

100. Which type of cipher involves a permutation of the letters?

a. Substitution Cipher
b. Transposition Cipher
c. Polyalphabetic Cipher
d. One-Time Pad

Questions and Answers

1. In a typical switch, where is information about Layer 2 addressing stored?

   a. L2 Table
   b. CAM Table
   c. MAC Address Table
   d. Routing Table

Correct Answer: c

Explanation: In order to forward frames, a switch will reference the MAC address table. This table contains information about Layer 2 addressing, such as the hardware MAC addressing itself, and the correlating port.

2. Which protocol is used to provide quick, automatic addressing within a network?

   a. ARP
   b. DNS
   c. IP
   d. DHCP

Correct Answer: d

Explanation: A DHCP server can be used to issue unique IP addresses and automatically configure other network information. In a home or small business network, this is typically handled by a router. Larger enterprise networks may employ the use of a dedicated DHCP server.

3. What is the defining characteristic of a hub?

   a. They repeat information and transmit to peers
   b. They make intelligent forwarding decisions based on Layer 3 addressing
   c. They are more cost effective to deploy
   d. They use a MAC address table for frame switching

Correct Answer: a

Explanation: A hub simply acts as a repeater, copying the information received on a port and transmitting the information to all other available ports. Hubs are sometimes referred to as "bit spitters" because of this simple functionality.

4. Which category of Wireless Access Points (WAPs) are able to handle both real-time and management functions?

    a. Lightweight Access Points
    b. Autonomous Access Points
    c. Wireless LAN Controllers
    d. Wireless Repeaters

Correct Answer: b

Explanation: Autonomous Access Points are able to handle both real-time and management functions by themselves without the need of a Wireless LAN Controller (WLC). Real-time functions include transmission and encryption of frames, while management functions include things such as wireless channel selection, security settings, and more. A typical wireless access point found in a home would most likely be this type of WAP.

5. Which of the following is not one of the values that comprises the 5-Tuple information found in NetFlow?

    a. Source Port
    b. Destination IP
    c. Protocol
    d. MAC Address

Correct Answer: d

Explanation: The 5-Tuple refers to a set of five values inside a TCP/IP connection which are of special interest to Network and Security Administrators. These five values are the source and destination ports, the source and destination IP addresses, and the protocol used.

6. Which of the following is true in regard to NetFlow vs. full-packet capture techniques?

    a. NetFlow requires more storage
    b. They utilize the same bandwidth
    c. NetFlow is more cost effective
    d. Full-packet capture is faster

Correct Answer: c

Explanation: In general, full-packet capture is considered less efficient than implementing NetFlow. Full-packet capture essentially doubles the bandwidth in a network, generating large amounts of data and storage concerns. This is also more bandwidth-intensive, essentially doubling the network traffic. NetFlow is the preferred and most cost-effective way to capture network data.

7. Which form of Network Address Translation (NAT) allows for connections to be initiated bidirectionally?

    a. Static NAT
    b. Dynamic NAT
    c. Policy NAT
    d. Port Address Translation

Correct Answer: a

Explanation: With Static NAT, a single private IP address is mapped to a single public IP address. This is commonly used in web hosting implementations, allowing for bidirectional connections to be initiated – both to and from the host.

8. In which mode of deployment for a Cisco Web Security Appliance (WSA) are the other network clients aware of the device's presence?

    a. Transparent Proxy Mode
    b. Explicit Proxy Mode
    c. Web Cache Mode
    d. Proxy Redirect Mode

Correct Answer: b

Explanation: When deployed in explicit proxy mode, the Cisco WSA is deployed in-line behind the firewall. Typically, the firewall is configured to only allow outbound traffic from the WSA. All client requests for external resources are routed through the WSA, so the clients are explicitly aware of the device's presence in the network.

9. Which CVSS version 3 metric measures the level of access that an attacker needs in order to successfully launch an attack?

    a. Attack Complexity

b. User Interaction
c. Attack Vector
d. Privileges Required

Correct Answer: d

Explanation: The Privileges Required (PR) metric measures the level of access privilege an attacker must possess in order to successfully exploit a vulnerability within a system or network.

10. A user on your network receives an email with a malicious attachment, but there is no indication that the file was interacted with in any way. Which category of the Diamond Model of Intrusion does this activity fall under?

a. Reconnaissance
b. Installation
c. Exploitation
d. Delivery

Correct Answer: d

Explanation: An email arrival containing a compromised attachment would fall under the Delivery activity thread of the Diamond Model of Intrusion. If the malicious file in question had been interacted with by the user (i.e. the user opened the file), the next threat phase of Exploitation would be reached.

11. Which of the following is true in regard to the Principle of Least Privilege?

a. It does not apply to managers
b. It is essentially the same as Separation of Duties
c. All users should have minimum access
d. It is only necessary in regard to employees

Correct Answer: c

Explanation: The Principle of Least Privilege states that all users should only have the level of access required to complete their job duties, and no more. This applies to programs, processes, and systems as well, particularly in regard to granting root access.

12. What is defined as any potential danger to an asset within an organization?

a. Exploit

b. Threat
c. Malicious Actor
d. Threat Agent

Correct Answer: b

Explanation: A threat is defined as any potential danger to an asset within an organization. Anything that is valuable to an organization would be considered an asset, including hardware, proprietary information, and the employees themselves. Threats are mitigated by countermeasures.

13. What is identified as an active entity used to place resource requests for access to passive entities?

a. Subject
b. Object
c. Control
d. User

Correct Answer: a

Explanation: When using access control measures, the Subject is considered to be the active entity. The Subject actively makes requests for access to an Object, which is the passive data entity. In between the Subject and the Object, we use access controls to regulate Subject-Object interactivity.

14. In which phase of the access control process is a user required to prove their identity?

a. Identification
b. Authentication
c. Authorization
d. Accounting

Correct Answer: b

Explanation: The authentication step is where a user will be required to prove their identity. This typically happens in one of three main ways – authentication by knowledge (passwords, PINs, etc.), authentication by ownership (physical key, token, etc.), or authentication by characteristic (fingerprints or other biometric features).

15. Which type of users are ultimately responsible for the overall security of an asset?

a. System Owners
b. Security Administrators
c. Senior Management
d. End Users

Correct Answer: c

Explanation: Although each of these user roles have a responsibility to care for asset security, the ultimate responsibility falls on Senior Management. Although they delegate tasks to others, they are responsible for everything that takes place within a company, and therefore must continually ensure that assets are being properly protected.

16. Which of the following methods of authentication could be considered examples of authentication by characteristic?

a. Server room key
b. Passphrase
c. RFID card
d. Fingerprints

Correct Answer: d

Explanation: The three main categories of authentication include authentication by knowledge, authentication by ownership, and authentication by characteristic. Physical server room keys and RFID cards would both be considered as authentication by ownership. A passphrase would be a form of authentication by knowledge. Fingerprints comprise the category of authentication by characteristic, along with other similar biometric features.

17. Which of the following is a feature of a typical Mobile Device Management (MDM) solution?

a. Call tracking
b. PIN code enforcement
c. Cloud backups
d. Speed dial

Correct Answer: b

Explanation: Mobile Device Management (MDM) solutions provide a way for administrators to control bring your own device (BYOD) deployments, such as tablets and mobile phones. They have several security features, including the abilities to force PIN code setup, detect out-of-date OS versions, and remotely lock and wipe lost or stolen devices.

18. Which type of penetration test involves a case where no information about networks and systems are provided beforehand?

    a. Black box testing
    b. White box testing
    c. Gray box testing
    d. Red hat testing

Correct Answer: a

Explanation: With black box testing, no information about the network or systems is provided prior to testing. This type of testing is typically performed by an outside contractor and mimics the role of an average threat actor with no internal knowledge of the target system.

19. Which of the following is not considered to be an advantage of Security Information and Event Management (SIEM) systems?

    a. Command line interface
    b. Ability to correlate redundant log entries
    c. Log search functionality
    d. Lower administrative overhead

Correct Answer: a

Explanation: All of the above are desirable and preferred features of SIEMs, except for command line interface. Instead, the graphical user interface (GUI) is what sets apart SIEMs from normal methods of log collection. They have the ability to correlate data into helpful charts and graphs for easy comprehension.

20. During which phase of the patch management process would you take into account any additional mitigation measures needed during rollout?

    a. Identification
    b. Prioritization
    c. Evaluation
    d. Updating

Correct Answer: c

Explanation: Once available patches have been identified, and the affected systems have been prioritized, the evaluation phase is used to determine if any additional controls or protection measures are needed during the patching phase. This could include additional, temporary firewall rules, or taking the system completely offline. Actions taken are dependent upon the severity of the vulnerability itself.

21. Which of the following is an example of an asymmetrical algorithm commonly used in our modern networks?

    a. DES
    b. 3DES
    c. AES
    d. RSA

Correct Answer: d

Explanation: RSA key pairs consist of a public key and a private key, using an asymmetrical algorithm. These key pairs are used in many places, including the creation of an encrypted VPN between two routers.

22. Which of the following is not considered to be a deprecated hash function?

    a. SHA-1
    b. SHA-2
    c. MD5
    d. DSA

Correct Answer: b

Explanation: DSA, MD5, and SHA-1 are all known to have successful collision attack methods against them. The recommended solution is the SHA-2 family, particularly SHA-384 and higher whenever possible.

23. Which of the following values would not commonly be found within a digital certificate?

    a. Domain name
    b. Public key
    c. DNS Server
    d. CA Signature

Correct answer: c

Explanation: Inside a digital certificate is typically found information about the identity of the verified device. This information includes things such as the fully-qualified domain name, their public key, and the signature of a valid Certificate Authority (CA).

24. Which method of IPsec implementation includes payload encryption?

    a. ESP
    b. AH
    c. VPN
    d. DSL

Correct Answer: a

Explanation: While Authentication Header (AH) only provides authentication means, Encapsulating Security Payload (ESP) provides both authentication and encryption of the payload. They both use the same algorithms while providing different coverage.

25. Which of the following VPN protocols provides data integrity, authentication, and encryption?

    a. L2TP
    b. GRE
    c. SSL
    d. MPLS

Correct Answer: c

Explanation: By themselves, the L2TP, GRE, and MPLS protocols do not provide data integrity, authentication, and encryption. From this list, only SSL provides all of these features. However, L2TP, GRE, and MPLS can be combined with IPsec or SSL in order to cover these important functions.

26. Which of the following is not part of the IKE Phase 1 policy set that is needed for an ISAKMP SA negotiation?

    a. Encryption
    b. Key
    c. Group
    d. Lifetime

Correct Answer: b

Explanation: The mnemonic HAGLE is a good way to remember the parts of the IKE Phase 1 policy set. These include the following:

H – Hashing Algorithm
A – Authentication
G – Group
L – Lifetime
E – Encryption

27. Which step of VPN negotiation creates an IPsec Security Association (SA) when completed?

   a. Main Mode
   b. Aggressive Mode
   c. IKE Phase 1
   d. IKE Phase 2

Correct Answer: d

Explanation: IKE version 1 has the ability to perform tunnel negotiation in main mode or aggressive mode. IKE version 2 combines these modes as a more streamlined method of negotiation. IKE Phase 1 creates an ISAKMP Security Association (SA) upon completion, while IKE Phase 2 creates an IPsec Security Association (SA) upon completion.

28. Which type of SSL VPN requires a browser-based connection method?

   a. Thin Client VPN
   b. Clientless VPN
   c. Site-to-Site VPN
   d. Full Tunnel VPN

Correct Answer: b

Explanation: Clientless VPNs only require the remote peer to have an SSL capable browser to access remote resources. Typically, users browse to the public IP address of the firewall or other VPN device, where they are able to authenticate and access a web portal with shared data or applications. This is most useful for simple file sharing and applications that do not require TCP-based communication.

29. Which of the following statements are true in regard to memory stacks and heaps?

   a. Heaps can allocate blocks of memory at any time

b. Stacks can allocate blocks of memory at any time
c. Stacks are best for dynamic memory allocation
d. Heaps are best for static memory allocation

Correct Answer: a

Explanation: Heaps have the ability to allocate a block of memory at any time and also free it at any time. For this reason, heaps are best for dynamic memory allocation, while stacks are best for static memory allocation.

30. What is the best description of a handle function in Windows OS?

a. API programmers change handles
b. Handles grant access rights to the OS
c. Hides real memory addresses from API users
d. Pointers and handles are the same concept

Correct Answer: c

Explanation: One of the main functions of a handle is to create an abstract reference to a resource. The handle table is used to correspond real memory locations from any API users.

31. In Windows, what are defined as a long-running application which operate in its own session?

a. Registry Key
b. Program
c. WMI
d. Service

Correct Answer: d

Explanations: Services are long-running applications which operate in their own session. Services are ideal for running things within a user security context, to make sure that specific services start/stop as needed for particular users. Windows Administrators can affect services through several means, including the Services snap-in and PowerShell.

32. Which of the following is considered to be a function of the Windows Registry?

a. Software registration
b. Loading device drivers
c. Backing up OS settings

d. Collecting logging information

Correct Answer: b

Explanation: A few of the functions of the Windows Registry are to set user environment variables, store OS parameters, and load device drivers.

33. In UNIX environments, what is the name of the first process started during the boot sequence?

    a. Parent
    b. Init
    c. Daemon
    d. Orphan

Correct Answer: b

Explanation: The Init process is the first process that begins during the boot sequence. This is also referred to as the Schedule process and has a process identifier (PID) value of 1. The Init process does not have a parent process, since it is the initial process during boot.

34. What type of process happens when a parent process is terminated, but the child process continues to function on its own?

    a. Step-Parent Process
    b. Zombie Process
    c. Orphan Process
    d. Daemon Process

Correct Answer: c

Explanation: An orphan process results when a parent process is terminated, leaving behind a functional child process that continues to operate on its own. Orphan processes are considered child processes of the initial boot process, known as the Init process.

35. Which is the following is true about Daemon processes?

    a. They run in the background
    b. They run in the foreground
    c. They manage OS upgrades
    d. They cannot be terminated

Correct Answer: a

Explanation: Of the choices, the first selection is correct. Daemons are processes that run in the background waiting to be initiated by some sort of trigger or condition. A mail daemon waiting for message arrival is a common example of this. Many of these daemon processes are started at boot, and they can be terminated or restarted just like any other process.

36. Which severity of Syslog would indicate something such as a kernel panic?

    a. Level 10
    b. Level 7
    c. Level 3
    d. Level 0

Correct Answer: d

Explanation: Syslog severity levels range from 0-7, with 0 being the highest level (Emergency). The levels are as follows:

Level 0 – Emergency
Level 1 – Alert
Level 2 – Critical
Level 3 – Error
Level 4 – Warning
Level 5 – Notice
Level 6 – Info
Level 7 – Debug

37. What type of malicious software typically comes in the form of malicious code inserted into a legitimate application?

    a. Worm
    b. Keylogger
    c. Ransomware
    d. Logic Bomb

Correct Answer: d

Explanation: Logic bombs come in the form of malicious code that is inserted into a legitimate application. They can be set off once specific conditions are met in a system, such as a specific date/time being reached, a percentage of the hard drive space taken up, or any number of other options.

38. Which of the following is Cisco's recommended solution for endpoint protection?

    a. Cisco WSA
    b. Cisco ESA
    c. Cisco AMP
    d. Cisco ASA

Correct Answer: c

Explanation: Cisco Advanced Malware Protection (AMP) for endpoints is used to prevent threats at the point of entry, and then continuously track every file it lets onto an endpoint. This solution also uncovers advanced threats such as ransomware and is considered to be a next-generation solution.

39. What is another name for a host-based firewall?

    a. Next-Generation Firewall
    b. Personal Firewall
    c. Standard Firewall
    d. Stateful Firewall

Correct Answer: b

Explanation: A host-based firewall is also referred to as a personal firewall. These types of firewalls are software-based solutions which provide Layer 3 and 4 protection. Although these are not a catch-all solution, they are an important part of a layered security approach.

40. What is the definition of a graylist item?

    a. Entities or actions not yet deemed to be either malicious or allowed
    b. Authorized hosts, applications, services, or email addresses
    c. Unauthorized hosts, applications, services, or email addresses
    d. Entities or actions that should be ignored completely

Correct Answer: a

Explanation: Graylist items are entities that have not yet been deemed to be malicious (a blacklist entities) or allowed (whitelist items). They sit in between blacklist and whitelist entities, hence the name. These entities can be moved into the whitelist or blacklist as deemed appropriate by the user.

41. Which type of security device has the ability to actively interact with network traffic and drop anything that has been deemed malicious?

    a. WPS
    b. IDS
    c. IPS
    d. ESA

Correct Answer: c

Explanation: An Intrusion Prevention System (IPS) sits in-line with all network traffic flow, typically behind the firewall. This device actively monitors traffic through deep inspection and can actively drop any traffic deemed as harmful. This active function is an advantage over legacy Intrusion Detection Systems (IDS), which are only able to detect and alert about issues without taking any action against the traffic.

42. Why is it important to enable the Network Time Protocol (NTP) on all devices within the network, particularly those from which logs are being collected?

    a. To make sure OS updates are applied
    b. To make sure logs are accurate
    c. For certificate management
    d. To synchronize network changes

Correct Answer: b

Explanation: In order to make sure log entries are accurate, it is critical to enable the Network Time Protocol (NTP) on network devices in order to obtain automatic time configuration. Logs will not be helpful if they are not factually accurate. Inaccurate time stamps can also create a challenge when collecting from multiple sources centrally, as they will be much harder to correlate the order of any incidents or events.

43. Under which directory do most UNIX-based systems keep logs?

    a. /var/log
    b. /var/syslog
    c. /var/lastlog
    d. /var/auth

Correct Answer: a

Explanation: In many Unix-based systems, the log directory is found under the /var/log file path. Many of the text-based logs will end with the *.log* identifier and can be viewed with a text editor.

44. Which of the following is not a useful attribute that you would want to collect during endpoint monitoring?

    a. Service pack data
    b. Application logs
    c. DNS hostnames
    d. Running processes

Correct Answer: a

Explanation: Important attributes that you would want to collect for endpoint monitoring would include application logs, IP addresses, DNS hostnames, geolocation data, and running processes, to name a few.

45. Which Cisco product offers a solution to the challenge of identifying attack information where Network Address Translation (NAT) is deployed?

    a. Cisco AMP for Endpoints
    b. Cisco ASA with Firepower
    c. Intrusion Prevention System
    d. Cisco Lancope Stealthwatch

Correct Answer: d

Explanation: Cisco Lancope Stealthwatch has a NAT stitching feature, which can use NetFlow data with other network information in order to correlate translated IP addresses.

46. Which of the following is a common method for data exfiltration that uses data transfer via a protocol that is not designed for carrying data?

    a. Port Address Translation
    b. DNS Tunneling
    c. Backdoors
    d. Trojan Horse

Correct Answer: b

Explanation: Because the DNS protocol was not initially designed for data transfer, it is typically less inspected in terms of security monitoring. Attackers have developed ways to encode data into DNS packet payloads in order to exfiltrate private data out of a network. Many next-generation security appliances have the ability to detect this type of attack.

47. Which of the following would not be a red flag in regard to suspicious host activity on a network?

    a. High bandwidth usage for a specific endpoint
    b. Network activity at strange times
    c. Peer-to-peer communication
    d. Sluggish performance on the host

Correct answer: d

Explanation: While all of the options would be cause for some concern, sluggish local performance is not always an indicator or suspicious network activity in the way that the other three scenarios would be.

48. What is Tor primarily used for?

    a. Local drive encryption
    b. Remote host management
    c. Anonymous browsing
    d. VPN functionality

Correct Answer: c

Explanation: Tor is a free tool that allows users to anonymously browse the web. Tor encrypts the application layer of a communication protocol stack multiple times, and then relays the data through several randomly selected Tor relays. Inside the encrypted data is the next node destination IP address, all encrypted within a separate layer that is hidden from all other nodes. The end of the chain is the exit node, where the encrypted traffic exits to the public internet destination. This tool is used both for legitimate anonymity reasons, and also as a masking tool for threat actors.

49. Which of the following intelligence gathering sources would not be considered a passive reconnaissance method?

    a. Port scan
    b. DNS lookup

c. Search engines
d. Social media

Correct Answer: a

Explanation: DNS lookups, search engines, and social media sites are all considered to be open source intelligence gathering methods, which use passive reconnaissance techniques. Port scanning is one of several active reconnaissance methods, where an attacker is actively interacting directly with a target network.

50. Which type of attack utilizes networks of compromised hosts to render target networks or systems unavailable?

   a. Zombies
   b. DoS
   c. DDoS
   d. Ransomware

Correct Answer: c

Explanation: Denial of Service (DoS) attacks involve a single computer or connection, whereas Distributed Denial of Service (DDoS) attacks utilize multiple computers or connections. Often these are controlled by a botnet system, which is a network of hosts that have been compromised and fallen under the control of a threat actor.

51. Which tenet of the CIA triad is encryption used to protect?

   a. Confidentiality
   b. Integrity
   c. Availability
   d. Authorization

Correct Answer: a

Explanation: The primary method for protecting asset confidentiality is through the use of encryption. Encryption ensures that only the intended audience is able to read or interpret data.

52. Which of the following is not included in the DREAD threat modeling methodology?

   a. Damage Potential
   b. Reconnaissance

c. Exploitability
d. Affected Users

Correct Answer: b

The DREAD thread modeling framework consists of the following components:

D – Damage Potential
R – Reproducibility
E – Exploitability
A – Affected Users
D – Discoverability

53. Which of the following is not included in the STRIDE threat modeling methodology?

   a. Tampering
   b. Reputation
   c. Denial of Service
   d. Elevation of Privilege

Correct Answer: b

Explanation: The STRIDE threat modeling framework consists of the following components:

S – Spoofing
T – Tampering
R – Reproducibility
I – Information Disclosure
D – Denial of Service
E – Elevation of Privilege

54. What is the sum of all pathways or means by which an attacker can gain access to a resource?

   a. Attack Vector
   b. Entry Point
   c. Injection Point
   d. Attack Surface

Correct Answer: d

Explanation: An attack vector is defined as a pathway or means by which an attacker can gain access to a resource. Any typical network has numerous attack vectors, ranging from laptops and mobile devices to email accounts. The sum of all attack vectors within a network is defined as the attack surface.

55. What is defined as conditions that must exist beyond an attacker's control in order to exploit a vulnerability?

    a. Availability
    b. Exposure
    c. Complexity
    d. Vector

Correct Answer: c

Explanations: Complexity cases the need for further reconnaissance or system exceptions in order for a successful attack to take place. Low complexity means that few limitations are in place, while high complexity means that more effort will be required to compromise a system or network.

56. Which CVSS metric measures the need for actions to be taken from someone other than the threat actor?

    a. User Interaction
    b. Privileges Required
    c. Assistance Vector
    d. Scope Change

Correct Answer: a

Explanation: This is essentially the measure of whether or not a threat actor can carry out a successful attack without the assistance of an end user. As an example, a phishing email attempt would require user interaction. The simple arrival of the phishing message itself would not perform any malicious action or gain any privileges. First, user interaction would be required, most likely in the form of a user clicking a malicious file or link attached to the message.

57. Which type of forensic investigation is categorized as a typical corporate investigation?

    a. Individual Investigation
    b. Private Investigation
    c. Public Investigation
    d. Criminal Investigation

Correct Answer: b

Explanation: Private investigations are also known as corporate investigations. These investigate incidents relevant to the employer which are not illegal but may warrant discipline or termination. If any illegal activity is discovered during a private investigation, the scope changes to that of a public investigation and may require intervention from law enforcement.

58. In regard to cyber forensics, what is defined as the process of searching through unallocated hard drive space in order to attempt deleted file recovery?

   a. Write Blocking
   b. Disk Imaging
   c. Data Carving
   d. Drive Hashing

Correct Answer: c

Explanation: During a forensic investigation, it's very common to make a bit-for-bit copy of any drive being investigated, including the unallocated space on the drive. Forensic tools such as EnCase can attempt deleted data file recovery, a process known as data carving.

59. What is the term for a basic unit that an Operating System allocated processor time toward?

   a. Service
   b. Job
   c. Thread
   d. Object

Correct Answer: c

Explanation: Threads are the building blocks of the Operating System processes, which provides resources for programs. Thread pools are groups of threads that work together and reduce the management requirements in a system.

60. Which of the following would not be considered a common cyber-attack artifact element?

   a. IP address
   b. URL
   c. Hashes
   d. VPN

Correct Answer: d

Explanation: Common artifact elements that can be left behind in the event of a security incident include IP addresses, host names, domain names, URLs, client and server ports, system API calls, hashes, and file or registry information. One step towards collecting artifacts is a centralized logging system that leverages NetFlow data.

61. In terms of alerting, what does it mean when there is malicious activity within our systems being seen as legitimate actions?

    a. False Positives
    b. False Negatives
    c. True Negatives
    d. True Positives

Correct Answer: b

Explanation: The ultimate goal of our alerting is to only receive True Positives and True Negatives. False Positives would be when legitimate activity is incorrectly identified as malicious action. False Negatives are the opposite and are described in the question – when there is malicious activity being seen as legitimate.

62. Which of the following is not a common type of evasion technique used against traditional IDS and IPS?

    a. Jumbo Frames
    b. Fragmentation
    c. Encryption
    d. Low Bandwidth

Correct Answer: a

Explanation: Evasion techniques known to be successful against traditional IDS and IPS include fragmentated packets, low bandwidth attacks, address spoofing, and payload encryption. Most next-generation devices have mitigation techniques in place to stop these known attacks.

63. Which protocol is used by IPFIX for transport of packets?

    a. SSL
    b. SCTP
    c. HTTPS

d. ESP

Correct Answer: b

Explanation: Stream Control Transmission Protocol (SCTP) operates at the transport layer and serves a role similar to TCP and UDP. This is sometimes referred to as next-generation TCP, or TCPng.

64. Which version of NetFlow is the IPFIX flow standard based upon?

   a. NetFlow Version 9
   b. NetFlow Version 8
   c. NetFlow Version 7
   d. NetFlow Version 5

Correct Answer: a

Explanation: IPFIX is based on NetFlow Version 9. IPFIX is an IETF standard specifically meant to open up flow to a broad range of vendors more easily, as opposed to the NetFlow protocol developed specifically by Cisco.

65. What does the National Institute of Security and Technology (NIST) define as an observable occurrence in a system or a network?

   a. Violation
   b. Incident
   c. Event
   d. Breach

Correct Answer: c

Explanation: An event is defined by NIST as any observable occurrence in a system or a network. This is not inherently good or bad, as an event can be either. If an event leads to negative consequences, such as system crashes, packet floods, unauthorized usage, or any number or other things, these are categorized as adverse events.

66. What does the National Institute of Security and Technology (NIST) define as a violation or imminent threat of violation of computer security policies, acceptable use policies, or standard security practices?

   a. Security Event
   b. Breach

c. Negative Event

d. Security Incident

Correct Answer: d

Explanation: Examples of security incidents can range from denial of service conditions caused by botnet attacks to the accidental exposure of sensitive information through phishing. Any attack that compromises personal or business data would be considered a security incident.

67. Which of the following is not part of the Incident Response Life Cycle as outlined by NIST?

a. Preparation

b. Detection and Analysis

c. System Backups

d. Post-Incident Activity

Correct Answer: c

Explanation: The four phases of the Incident Response Life Cycle as outlined by NIST special publication 800-61 are as follows:

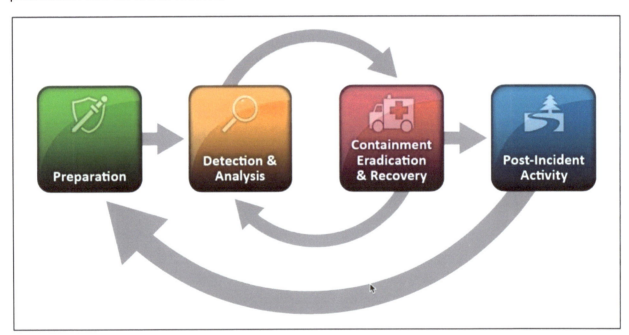

68. Which of the following is considered to be a main goal of Computer Security Incident Response Teams (CSIRTs)?

a. Hiring penetration testers

b. Monitoring firewall rules

c. Minimize damage to assets

d. Deploy intrusion prevention systems

Correct Answer: c

Explanation: One of the main goals of a typical CSIRT is to contain damage and mitigate security incidents. They also provide guidance for mitigation and work to prevent any future occurrences.

69. Which type of team is typically formed by hardware and software vendors to investigate, resolve, and disclose security vulnerabilities in their own products.

a. PSIRTs

b. CERTs

c. CSIRTs

d. FIRSTs

Correct Answer: a

Explanation: These duties outline the job description of a typical Product Security Incident Response Team (PSIRT). For example, Cisco's own internal PSIRT team has a blog dedicated to disclosing vulnerabilities in their own technologies, for the purpose of consumer awareness. PRISTs use the Common Vulnerability Scoring System (CVSS) Version 3 to provide vulnerability severity ratings.

70. The PCI DSS framework was developed to protect which of the following?

a. Electronic healthcare information

b. Financial Data

c. Tax Returns

d. Voter Registration

Correct Answer: b

Explanation: The Payment Cared Industry Data Security Standard (PCI DSS) is an information security standard for any organization that handles payment cards. This includes merchants, financial institutions, and developers who create processing software. Information protected includes the financial data found in the card chip and the magnetic strip.

71. Which of the following is not a phase of the Cyber Kill Chain?

a. Recovery

b. Installation

c. Exploitation

d. Reconnaissance

Correct Answer: a

Explanation: The Cyber Kill Chain contains the following seven steps:

1. Reconnaissance
2. Weaponization
3. Delivery
4. Exploitation
5. Installation
6. Command and Control (C2)
7. Actions

72. In the Diamond Model of Intrusion, what is identified as the target that is being exploited?

a. Infrastructure

b. Adversary

c. Vulnerability

d. Victim

Correct Answer: d

Explanation: The four pieces identified by the Diamond Model of Intrusion are the Adversary, Infrastructure, Capabilities, and Victim. The Victim identifies the target that is being exploited.

73. What kind of forensic evidence is considered to be the most reliable when attempting to arrive at an analytical assertion?

a. Corroborative

b. Indirect

c. Direct

d. Circumstantial

Correct Answer: c

Explanation: Direct evidence is based on observation or fact and is the more reliable for arriving at a conclusion. In the event that a private investigation turns into a public criminal investigation, this type of evidence holds the most weight in court.

74. Which tenet of the CIA triad refers to the trustworthiness and veracity of information?

    a. Confidentiality
    b. Integrity
    c. Availability
    d. Encryption

Correct Answer: b

Explanation: Integrity involves maintaining the consistency, accuracy, and trustworthiness of data over its entire life cycle. This includes data in all states, whether at rest or in motion.

75. During which phase of the Cyber Kill Chain is the adversary actively in the network, beginning to achieve objectives?

    a. Weaponization
    b. Installation
    c. Delivery
    d. Actions

Correct Answer: d

Explanation: The actions phase can include things such as actively stealing data, listening to network traffic, or reserving a compromised system as part of a larger overall scheme. An attacker may begin to pivot to other systems, or to start the chain all over again from inside the network.

76. What does PHI stand for?

    a. Private Health Information
    b. Protected Health Information
    c. Personal Health Information
    d. Private Health Insurance

Correct Answer: b

Explanation: Protected Health Information (PHI) under the US law is any information about health status, provision of health care, or payment for health care that is created or collected by a covered entity. This information can be linked to a specific individual and broadly includes any part of a patient's medical record or payment history.

77. What is the measure of the actual amount of data traveling through a network?

a. Throughput
b. Bandwidth
c. Speed
d. Latency

Correct Answer: a

Explanation: Often the terms bandwidth and throughput are confused. Bandwidth is the measure of the maximum amount of data that can travel through a specific point in a network, usually measured in bits per second (BPS). Throughput is how much data is actually traveling through that point, and at what speed.

78. In regard to baseline network metrics, what might be an indicator of a potentially underutilized area of a network topology?

a. Peaks
b. Valleys
c. Dips
d. Latency

Correct Answer: b

Explanation: When you have good baseline metrics for normal traffic in your network, peaks or valleys above the baseline can be indicative of potential issues. Valleys may indicate underutilization, or even failure in the case of valleys reaching all the way to zero unexpectedly. Peaks indicate spikes in throughput that may bring delays in traffic, or even loss of data packets.

79. What type of memory gets allocated during compile time by a program?

a. Static
b. Startup
c. Random
d. Dynamic

Correct Answer: a

Explanation: Static memory allocation happens when a program allocates memory at compile time.

80. Which of the following is not one of the three general types of forensic evidence?

a. Best Evidence

b. Corroborating Evidence
c. Digital Evidence
d. Circumstantial Evidence

Correct Answer: c

Explanation: The three general types of evidence are best evidence, corroborating evidence, and circumstantial evidence (also known as indirect evidence).

81. What common type of attack is stored on the web server itself, and is accomplished through submitting input to forms which populate database fields, such as comment boxes or message boards?

a. Reflected XSS
b. SQL Injection
c. Phishing
d. Persistent XSS

Correct Answer: d

Explanation: Persistent Cross-Site Scripting (XSS) occurs when data provided by the attacker is saved by the web server itself, then permanently displayed to other users in the course of regular browsing. Unlike Non-Persistent XSS, Persistent XSS Does not require a social engineering phase for delivery.

82. What is the Syslog severity level for debug messages?

a. 2
b. 3
c. 7
d. 5

Correct Answer: c

Explanation: Syslog severity levels are as follows:

Level 0 – Emergency
Level 1 – Alert
Level 2 – Critical
Level 3 – Error
Level 4 – Warning
Level 5 – Notice

Level 6 – Info

Level 7 – Debug

83. What is defined as a set of rules related to encrypting or decrypting data?

   a. Key
   b. Cipher
   c. Algorithm
   d. Encryption

Correct Answer: b

Explanation: When using a cipher, the original information is known as plaintext, and the encrypted form is referred to as ciphertext.

84. Which of the following is not an important consideration under the Sarbanes-Oxley (SOX) Act framework?

   a. C-Level employees must certify financial records
   b. External auditors must perform annual audits
   c. Public disclosure of changes to financial conditions
   d. Annual corporate shareholder meetings

Correct Answer: d

Explanation: The SOX Act was created to protect investors by improving the accuracy and reliability of corporate actions and finances. This act essentially was created to crack down on corporate fraud and restore the faith of stock market investors.

85. Which type of solution is used as a collection of procedures detailing security operations, such as identifying, containing, and removing threats?

   a. Runbook
   b. Procedure Guide
   c. Instruction Manual
   d. Policy

Correct Answer: a

Explanation: Runbooks can be thought of as instruction manuals for all of our operations, and also for incident identification and response. There are many software solutions which help to automate Runbook creation and create searchable information repositories. Examples include RunDeck and Cisco Workload Automation.

86. What type of network-related symptom is defined as a periodical, outbound connection that comes from a compromised host?

    a. Beaconing
    b. Homing
    c. Pinging
    d. Calling

Correct Answer: a

Explanation: Beaconing can be a sign of a compromised host in a network. This can indicate that an internal client is communicating with an external host and may actively be under the control of an attacker. This is frequently seen in malware and is referred to as Command and Control (C2). This is effective because many firewalls are much less restrictive with outbound traffic.

87. Which type of password attack tool uses a large database with hash values pre-matched to plain text outputs?

    a. Dictionary Attack
    b. Brute-Force Attack
    c. Rainbow Table Attack
    d. Key-Logger Attack

Correct Answer: c

Explanation: Rainbow tables are a type of pre-computed password attack. Dictionary and Brute-Force attacks attempt to enter a password into the locked program, and the program then hashes the entry and compares the hash to the correct password hash. Rainbow Table Attacks use a table of passwords that have already been hashed.

88. Which type of common wireless attack uses a rogue access point that appears to be legitimate, typically placed in a public area with open authentication?

    a. Eavesdropping
    b. Evil Twin Attack
    c. MAC Spoofing
    d. Management Jacking

Correct Answer: b

Explanation: An Evil Twin is a fraudulent wireless access point that appears to be legitimate but is instead setup to eavesdrop on client traffic. Using an Evil Twin in a public place disguised as a free hotspot is the most common way to perform such an attack.

89. Which of the following procedures would not be helpful when collecting data for measuring network throughput?

    a. SPAN port configuration
    b. NetFlow collector data
    c. Gateway firewall statistics
    d. Operating System versions

Correct Answer: d

Explanation: All of the above would be helpful information to have when assessing throughput statistics, other than OS versions.

90. Which analysis type is based on known facts obtained about the incident, breach, or infection?

    a. Behavioral
    b. Contextual
    c. Probabilistic
    d. Deterministic

Correct Answer: d

Explanation: Deterministic analysis is performed using hard facts. These are obtained by various methods and devices, including NetFlow data collection, log examination, port mirroring, and other methods. This is also referred to as First Party Data.

91. Which of the following is not considered to be one of the important meta-features used in the Diamond Model of Intrusion?

    a. Timestamp
    b. Result
    c. Password
    d. Methodology

Correct Answer: c

Explanation: Meta -features in the Diamond Model of Intrusion provide useful context for an incident. They include important metrics as they relate to the incident itself, such as timestamps, results, direction, methodology, and resources.

92. Which of the following would be an example of an external entity that you may be required to communicate with during the investigation and resolution of a security incident?

    a. Media
    b. Managers
    c. Employees
    d. Financial Advisors

Correct Answer: a

Explanation: The best example in this list of a potential external entity that may require communication is the media. NIST publication 800-61 outlines several areas that may require external communication depending on your industry, as seen below. For example, HIPAA violations may require communication with customers, media, and law enforcement agencies.

93. Which of the following data artifacts are not commonly shown in NetFlow records?

    a. Source Ports

b. Usernames
c. Destination IP Addresses
d. Protocols

Correct Answer: b

Explanation: Usernames are not part of NetFlow data. The critical parts of the NetFlow 5-Tuple are source and destination port, source and destination IP address, and the protocol.

94. NIST SP 800-61 outlines the important phases of a security incident, including the post-incident activity phase. Which of the following procedures is not considered to be part of this post-mortem?

a. Discussing lessons learned
b. Retaining evidence
c. Pinpointing attacking hosts
d. Using collected data

Correct Answer: c

Explanation: Critical pieces of the post-incident activity phase as outlined by NIST SP 800-61 include stating lessons learned, using collected incident data, and making considerations for evidence retention.

95. When encapsulating data using the OSI model as a reference, the MAC address of the sending and receiving hosts are identified at which layer?

a. Layer 4
b. Layer 3
c. Layer 2
d. Layer 7

Correct Answer: c

Explanation: Layer 2 is the data link layer of the OSI model. This layer receives packets from the Network Layer and places them on the network medium, such as cable or wireless. The data link layer encapsulates each packet in a frame and the MAC header carries the source and destination MAC addresses.

96. Which of the following is not a common message exchanged during the four-step DHCP address negotiation between server and client?

a. DHCPDISCOVER
b. DHCPOFFER
c. DHCPREQUEST
d. DHCPRENEW

Correct Answer: d

Explanation: DHCP clients obtain a DHCP lease containing network information in a four-step process:

1. DHCPDISCOVER: The client broadcasts a request for a DHCP server.
2. DHCPOFFER: DHCP servers on the network offer an address to the client.
3. DHCPREQUEST: The client broadcasts a request to lease an address from one of the offering DHCP servers.
4. DHCPACK: The DHCP server acknowledges the client, assigns DHCP options, and updates its DHC database.

97. Which type of device sits between protected and unprotected networks in order to terminate connections as a "middle-man" between the two?

a. Proxy
b. Firewall
c. IPS
d. Relay

Correct Answer: a

Explanation: More common in the early Internet days, a proxy is a point-to-point connection between a trusted and untrusted network. Rather than having dedicated proxy servers as a security measure these days, many next-generation devices have proxy functionalities bundled in. This allows a way to employ monitoring and content-filtering on a network.

98. Which of the following is not an example of a well-known symmetric-key algorithm?

a. 3DES
b. Blowfish
c. RSA
d. AES

Correct Answer: c

Explanation: The Rivest-Shamir-Adleman (RSA) algorithm is one of the first public-key cryptosystems, using an asymmetric key pair. 3DES, Blowfish, and AES are all common examples of symmetric algorithms.

99. In Linux, which of the following commands is used to change group ownership of a particular file?

    a. CHmod
    b. CHgrp
    c. CHown
    d. CHedit

Correct Answer: b

Explanation: The CHmod command changes individual file permissions, CHgrp is used to change the group ownership, and CHown changes the file's individual owner.

100. Which type of cipher involves a permutation of the letters?

    a. Substitution Cipher
    b. Transposition Cipher
    c. Polyalphabetic Cipher
    d. One-Time Pad

Correct Answer: b

Explanation: Whereas Substitution ciphers replace each letter with a different letter or symbol to produce the ciphertext, in a Transposition cipher, the letters are just moved around. One important strength of transposition ciphers is that they are not susceptible to frequency analysis, since we have not changed the symbols for each letter.

Recommended Study Resource

To supplement your studies, Charles Judd has created a video training series that covers key topics from the CCNA Cyber Ops SECFND 210-250 and SECOPS 210-255 exams. The training includes 137 individual videos with a run time of over 10 Hours. All of the training videos are available for downloadable offline usage.

Learn more about the **Cisco CCNA Cyber Ops Video Training Series** here:

https://kwtrain.com/cyberops

Keep in Touch with Us

I am deeply honored that you've trusted me to help you prepare for your exam. If you have found value in this study resource, please leave a review on Amazon.com.

If you would like to keep in contact with us, or explore other video trainings that we offer, please visit our website: **https://kwtrain.com**

You can also follow Kevin Wallace Training on our various social media channels:

Twitter: http://twitter.com/kwallaceccie

Facebook: http://facebook.com/kwallaceccie

YouTube: http://youtube.com/user/kwallaceccie

LinkedIn: http://linkedin.com/in/kwallaceccie

Google+: http://google.com/+KevinWallace

Snapchat: kwallaceccie

About the Author

Charles Judd, Technical Instructor

CCNA Security and R&S | BS Network Security | AS Applied Technology & Machine Technology

Charles works for Kevin Wallace Training as a content developer and technical instructor. His real-world experience includes a decade of CNC programming and operation, duties as a Network Engineer for a healthcare and HIPAA compliancy-focused MSP, and freelance Graphic/Web Designing and IT Consulting.

Charles currently creates video training courses and writes books on networking technologies (**https://kwtrain.com/products**). He lives in central Kentucky with his wife Jeanna and their three sons - Caleb, Cameron and Corey.